Praise for *Many To Remember*

Rachel Kaufman's lucid, alchemical poems turn the history of her family and crypto-Jews into myth that is at once fixed and unfixed, tenuous and lasting. Her poems reckon with rather than solve contradictions: survivors disinterested in their history, Jews who are refugees and colonizers, words that fail to express. Yet at times her myth's contradictions and instability are a force of meaning: *I realized there/was only/land and storm leaning/into earth,/breaking the soil/into pieces so/it could claim/at sunrise/its mending.* Kaufman's book is essential reading to all contrarians grappling with their histories.   —EMILY WARN

I want to say that, by its nature, poetry is one way that the present discovers its possibilities through a dialogue with the past. In *Many to Remember,* Rachel Kaufman enacts that persistent struggle to uncover the living presence of history as we try to forge a life in the everyday. Writes the poet, "At the edge of words/I accompany you, seeing," and her poems are a company we can trust, a way of seeing we can believe in. This is a startling debut.   —RICHARD DEMING

MANY TO REMEMBER

Rachel Kaufman

DOS MADRES

2021

DOS MADRES PRESS INC.

P.O. Box 294, Loveland, Ohio 45140

www.dosmadres.com   editor@dosmadres.com

Dos Madres is dedicated to the belief that the small press is essential to the vitality of contemporary literature as a carrier of the new voice, as well as the older, sometimes forgotten voices of the past. And in an ever more virtual world, to the creation of fine books pleasing to the eye and hand.

Dos Madres is named in honor of Vera Murphy and Libbie Hughes, the "Dos Madres" whose contributions have made this press possible.

Dos Madres Press, Inc. is an Ohio Not For Profit Corporation and a 501 (c) (3) qualified public charity. Contributions are tax deductible.

Executive Editor: Robert J. Murphy

Illustration & Book Design: Elizabeth H. Murphy
www.illusionstudios.net

Cover & section graphics are adapted from "Portamento"
© Elanna Bernstein, used by permission of the artist.

Typeset in Adobe Garamond Pro & Arcitectura
ISBN 978-1-953252-23-4
Library of Congress Control Number: 2021933789

p.vii: Seal - Image Courtesy of The American Jewish Historical Society.

p.x: Title page from Mexican Inquisition Documents: 1595 Mexico City, Leonor de Carvajal, BANC MSS 96/95 m v.3, The Bancroft Library, University of California, Berkeley.

First Edition

ACKNOWLEDGEMENTS

I am deeply grateful for the editors of the following publications in which some of these poems first appeared: *Harvard Review Online, Southwestern American Literature, Western Humanities Review, JuxtaProse, The Raw Art Review, Levee Magazine, Kalliope, Connecticut Best Emerging Poets,* and *Good Works Review.* "New Mexico Lightning" received the Academy of American Poets Sean T. Lannan Poetry Prize, and "Burial" received honorable mention in the Charles Bukowski Prize for Poetry. Thank you to the archivists at the American Jewish Historical Society, the Bancroft Library, and the Center for Southwest Research at the University of New Mexico for their knowledge and conversation.

As Baba says, my cup runneth over.

To have generations to write to and for is an honor and a blessing. Grandma, Grandpa, Baba, and Zede, thank you for setting a place for me.

This book is for my parents, who built a home of song and light to hold us, and who still keep their children's artwork on the walls.

Thank you to my many generous teachers whose words and wisdom are marked in these pages and to Dos Madres Press, Robert and Elizabeth, for their faith and kindness.

To all the teachers and friends I have stumbled upon in the desert, in the archive, on the way—it's difficult to imagine more generous hands to guide me.

for Mira
and Miriam

TABLE OF CONTENTS

Preface: Rooting Down......................1

I Inquisitors
New Mexico Lightning......................9
Observant Marranos......................10
Inquisition Letters......................13
Trial Number 23 (Translation)..........15
Me'am Lo'ez..............................16
Prophetess...............................17

II New Origin Myths
The Myth of la Llave......................21
Testament................................23
Mother of Exile..........................25
If Hunger Persuades......................26
At These Limits..........................28
Prophets.................................29
Many to Remember........................31
New Origin Myth..........................32

III Myth Expands

(Flush Inspired)................................35
Illusion!...37
Idols in the Desert...........................38
God's Desert....................................39
The Shul in Chelm...........................41
Reflection over Winter.....................43
Collecting Samples..........................44
Burial..45

IV Archive's Tales

Manuscript......................................49
Archive's Tales I..............................51
Archive's Tales II.............................52
Animal Markings..............................53
Unearth...55
Holy Wilderness..............................56
Archive's Diction.............................58

V Behind the Brush

Translation......................................61
He Fell Again...................................62
Cossacks Coming.............................66
Zede, Rachel....................................67
Behind the Brush.............................70
Libro de Cordilleras.........................71

Epilogue

[re-]Exodus.....................................74

Notes...77
About the Author.............................81

MANY TO REMEMBER

El s.^{do} p.^{rocesso} g.^{ra}

Doña Leonor de Caruajal n.^l
de Benauente en los Rey.^{os} de Castilla muo. de Jorge de
Almeyda Portugues hija de Fran.^{co} Rodriguez de Matos
Relaxado en estatua por la ley de Moysen y de doña Fran.^{ca}
de Caruajal reconciliada por lo mismo

N.º 8 A.

Vista .M.
Man. prender
Prission en Mex.^{co}
Monición.^{es} 1. 2.ª 3.^a
Acusacion,
Aprueua,
Publicacion
3.ª diff.^{on}

Iudaia ante relapsa

Abogado y cura.^{or}

El lic.^{do} Guspar de Valdes

Votada.

A relaxar
seglar concon̄

Ley. 2.º

X

PREFACE
Rooting Down

Zede, grandfather. Baba, grandmother. Grandma and
Grandpa, translated. Do not count your loved ones, says
Baba, Baruch HaShem.

Inquisición, trial and fire. Exiles, borders half-open, Spain
to Mexico to New Mexico. Pack your keys, scrolls, shiny
new crucifix. Shifting other bodies away, fleeing and
colonizing at once, it depends who you are. Inquisition
travels east to west, does not travel north. Converted
Jews flee, settle, flee. Crypto-Jews, secret Jews, practice in
hiding, transmit through objects, recall.

Zede, Zweibrücken, Germany, 1933. Connecticut, soon.
Baba, Southern Boulevard, Bronx. Her mother, Marjem
(soon Miriam) Kine, born Schnitzler, Bukowsko, Poland.
Fled, stranded for a while, picked up each language. Then
America, before Baba's birth. Grandma, Brooklyn. From
the Kirsch family, mother from the Zuckermans, Poland.
Grandpa, Brooklyn. Born to Sarah and Louis, Brooklyn.
Grandparents, Russia and Poland.

It is biblical law to mourn a spouse for thirty days
but to mourn a child or parent for one year. A *Plaza
Mayor*, everywhere I go and don't go. Each country, city,
conquered, and a little horse statue put up at its center.
Crypto-Jews watch, sometimes join in, undercover.

Grandma says she watched the *shochet* (butcher) swing the

1

chicken above his head. By its neck, it spouted red blood, made a map on the floor. To the dressmaker, soldiers' camp, pogrom ruins in the next town, barn door open, children's screams echo. Why so much echoing across our deserts and forests? Only the sea untouched, until ships stroked the horizon.

I was not a part of this Old World. Grandma was, barely. Baba, too. Barely as in yes, a trace, they remember. Colors and things.

Grandpa was elsewhere, kicking dust on his way home from Yeshiva. The middle of the day, he left his *tallis* at home, an excuse for a walk and less praying. He almost joined the Yankees (add that to the genealogy), but he'd already left for the army when they called. His mother picked up. She and her husband left with a note from their eighteen-year-old son—gone to war, something brief. Perhaps he envied the Old World, its seeing, fleeing, sorrow born and honored. Now he stays with Grandma in Florida, and they stay put. "Nothing's changed around here, and that's the way we like it!" Brooklyn and Bronx accents, phone with a spiral cord.

While Baba was in the Bronx, a house of three generations and one toilet, Zede was in Zweibrücken. My only grandparent not born here. Jewish, following the moon, learning how to spell and read. Not one word of German after they left. His father, Rabbi and Cantor Eleazar, didn't want to leave his congregation. My Zede's birth and Hitler's rise, time passed. On Kristallnacht, Eleazar was arrested, their apartment destroyed. Zede and his brother came home to soldiers, thought it great fun to toss their last papers, stamps, dishes out the broken window, now just a space to fall through. Zede tells this with barely a grimace, unimportant next to later loss.

They lived above a shop where a man sold beer. They had a nanny. Zede says he was hit by a car at five-years-old while crossing the street to greet her. "See it, here?" Zede's mother, Martha, got his father out of jail, gathered the home and children, crossed the French border. A soon-to-be war criminal, horrific deeds, drove them. A policeman who played chess with Eleazar. They crossed other borders alone. Eleazar sought papers in America, missed a ship that sank, boarded a ship with Wrong Way Corrigan.

Mother and children wandered, just like Baba's ancestor women one generation back. Baba's mother, Miriam, stayed in barns with roosters, her sisters, and her mother, Pearl. It took Pearl's husband six years to earn enough for the family's trip. "Were they faithful all that time?" "Oh yes, absolutely." Pearl told Baba these stories (auditoriums, cots, roosters) to get her to eat.

Mexico City, 1589, 1642, et al. No wives to get the men out of jail, children folding over, neighbors turning in neighbors. A legal hoax, each trial more redundant than the last. Not by hatred nor by enmity, sign here, but for the unloading of your soul. A red truck stacked with boxes. Menorahs? One God. Unload here, reload there. All I want, said Manuel Gomez de Acosta, Portuguese crypto-Jew, dead before his trial ended, is to be buried in white socks. White pants, white shirt, white socks, and a staff in my hand. They say he never asked for a rosary or a Latin book while he was sick. This is how they knew. Only lay in bed with his Jewish eyelids and prayed for white.

Generations later, families bury their relatives in white, write poems about martyred uncles and aunts, mirrors turned toward the walls. Whispers sweep across the dinner table, dust pushed out the door each Shabbos afternoon. The cemeteries are dead. How do we know? How do they know?

In jail, Luis de Carvajal el Mozo, famous crypto-Jew (Spain to Mexico, aboard his uncle's conquistador ship), sent letters to his sisters inside peach pits, banana skins. His letters are now a book. The archive remembers and forgets—myth, history, the weeping of each into the other.

"Las llaves de las puertas están en la cocina / para esconder secretos profundos de los cuartos....en una casa donde santos no miran por paredes / Raitos de luz escapan de la casita" // "The keys to the doors are in the kitchen / to hide the deep secrets of the rooms....in a house where saints do not look through walls / rays of light escape from inside" (*"Trancas Abiertas"* // "Opened Locks," Isabelle Medina Sandoval, 1995). The keys to old Spanish houses kept in cupboards, one day to return? The swallow, too, a symbol of the expelled Jew. Stories found in the kitchen.

Zede says he saw a Nazi parade as a young child, from afar. His father whisked him away, though he had brought him there, curious. Wanting to see.

《• •》

I am seeing two stories at once, overlaid, overlapping, distinct. Through each, the other—desert sun reflecting off scrolls. Empathy, rather than comparison.

For my great-grandparents, for theirs.

Santa Fe
March 2020

❮• | •❯
Inquisitors

Spanish graveyards, Hebrew-inscribed crosses, the Atlantic on ships. The records colonize west and Jews, now crypto-Jews, secret Jews, follow. Mexico City inquires, trials ensue. Children become priests, past-bearers, older priests. Marranos, they're called, pigs, New Christians, impure. Bread leavens in Santa Fe windowsills, hidden by curtains.

We form our myths like this—language leavened and recalled. Fable listens, unhinges, breaks loose, collecting the dust of our brooms.

New Mexico Lightning

falls like a candle
burning downwards
and out, bleats
into the canyon
old enough
to receive light
and not burn
When it bestows
upon rock redness
for its aging skin,
divides the sky
in slanted parts,
creates spirits
that reach
out their wings
to catch shards
(I bet the cacti
hear this each
night), dances needles
which fly off
its path in the dark—

on my drive to the sea
I realized there was only
land and storm leaning
into earth,
breaking the soil
into pieces so
it could claim
at sunrise
its mending.

Observant Marranos

The call of the blood, you say

and I nod my head,
the fall of the blood,

but no, you say,
the call of the blood,

and I nod my head and say,
yes, I hear, the flowing of blood

and you scream to me,
the calling of blood,

and I call to you,
the mud! it is falling,

blood is failing, all is crawling,
and you run off

and leave me with this language.

The call of mud,
the suds we use

to wipe clean
this blood of the past, or

this blood of desire
for either we wish

for clean blood, purity
of hand to foot to race,

or we remember
the weaving of desire with

kind, the desire for a kind,
for boxes filled

with a kind,
two kinds, at most.

The Marranos feel
the call of blood

back to their people, but
aren't they Jews

from the start?
Yes, the pamphlet

says and no,
the author inside

and with
out, a friend

and afraid, a cautious
touch to those

who sing
the same songs.

Lord of us all
or brown skin

he wonders to himself
as he writes

to kings and queens
for purses of gold.

Inquisition Letters

the legs put a lighthouse on
the hill the knees extended to form
a tree the world was created
by feet padding through time

the tree that formed was very tall
the lighthouse white and cracked
tiles sent over with imprints
by pigs' hooves to make them
tried (the hooves and tiles)
but some ran and didn't walk
and they cracked (the tiles and pigs)

in the desert the rain
brings up salt
then soil, so
following each storm
the farmers go out
and water the earth
back down

the ancient frail man is very
virtuous and helps
the farmers calling *bendita*
as they bend
over their fields
the woman opens up
as if land
accepting water

the letters brought news like this

words scratched on
peach and avocado pits
wrapped in taffeta
and hidden in melons, or
wrapped in ribbons and pocketed
inside banana's skin

the sweetest were meant
for the jailed man's favorite,
Doña Ana, or really
his favorite of those close by

his best sister remained
in a cell far away
with a darker woman
unable to send pits or pears
her hands traveled the wall
each day feigning engraving

a lute is playing
softly and its breeze
is mixing with the light
beneath her door
everyone is wearing hats
in the dark and counting
their days with ticks
on the palms of their hands
peaches all gone

Trial Number 23 (Translation)

To the first question, he says he knows
the questions asked and those
who ask them and he
is thirty years old and running
towards or away. To the second
question he says he has heard
the question and it contains
many people and it was said
by all of them at once and rang
in his ears. To the third question
he falls to the floor and smiles.
To the fourth he says he has never
heard of such lies or such questions
and only an answer like this
could resolve a question
like that. To the fifth
he says he does not know.
To the sixth he begins to denounce
every truth he believes and
his lies slip like silver.
To the seventh the audience
loses interest and he begins
to foam at the mouth.
There is no eighth and the people
and questions stream out
into the street and everyone
ties their shoes and he remains
insane, driven to
luckless admittance,
rain pouring down
his pointed hat.

Me'am Lo'ez

The winter nights are very
long, the cock crow turns
our beds to song, our house
is safe through words of prayer
which tangle, circle,
leave us there. We're told

our souls will grow
accustomed to hearing echoes
of our customs—these chantings
set apart from myth to keep
some holiness adrift.

It should be near but
not in hand, this spirit
which envelops land but never
touches down to rest, or settles
in our eager breath.

We're left with just one-
seventh of the light,
our words collapse
as awe loses sight.

Prophetess

I saw the oldest woman in the world
die today in Florida

in a pool of blue glass
ice cold, she said.

Her browned skin layered
in perfect circles

like the rings of a lake
expanding after interruption.

She walked like a swan
toes out, nose up

and it could be Egypt,
the desert, a Mexican plaza

lined with gold that held
her small feet

as she shuffled along.
The fish, dead, roll beneath

in water thin and clear,
washed up from bathhouses

and purity cellars
doorways inked

with secret symbols
and pigs' blood

soaking through the floor.

《• || •》
New Origin Myths

These myths are held, most true, in hands, tellings, homes. They sweep their kitchens, the crypto-Jews, engrave their stories in locked drawers.

Through birds, they recall—golondrina, swallow, expelled West. She falls to desert sand. They pick up feathers, hang them on walls. One day, perhaps, to return.

The Myth of la Llave

Don't you see the swallows
wilting in the sky
their wings fast asleep
on their backs.
The sparrow is fleeing
but the swallow is returning
golden key held
between beak and neck.
The old Spanish roads
wind through graveyards and mountains
following train tracks
as far as they will go.
They do not mind disruption
under their arching bells
light traveling through
patted and patched ground.
The swallows are buried underneath
their wings tied to their bellies with string,
the sparrows saw and hitched
their babies to their backs.
They are almost across the sea
but a yellow shadow in the water
mirrors their path
and they are distracted
homesick for red earth and pink clouds.
The light arcs back
to the buried towns and resting birds
who sit beneath the tracks.
Except for a few, the sparrows cease fleeing,

cling to shadow, and turn.
The swallows sigh and try
to fold the earth
more heavily over their heads.

Testament

As it is
the apple orchard burns

at dusk, red falling
from trees and sky.

By its shards, the margin
of the river, grass, splay

into a showing, swollen
then collapsed. The Bishop's

garden flowers over
the road, invites everyone

inside for tea and warm bread,
metal gates ornamented

in the old ways.
Swing hard

rusting iron, tall ceilings
leading to one point. Trapped?

All in good faith. Hands scramble
to open, break, evacuate

horses against a burning
backdrop. Do they take them

only to save themselves?
Danger inside, dampen

your shirt. Tilting bodies,
horse legs stuck in orchard

soil, branches drag
after the parade. Slowly,

they wind their way out,
up, on top of the hill,

they can see where smoke
ends, whispering into clear sky,

like seeing both ends
of a rainbow, testament

to the concert's horn,
harp, choir. To their east,

land overflowing, orchestral cacti
swaying past their place.

Mother of Exile

"The golondrina is always in search of her nest."
—Emma Moya's *Ode to the Wandering Swallow's Flight*,
University of New Mexico Archives

She is only and always in search of her nest.
Little jeweled creatures with tufts
on their heads, her babies coo and long
for bread. Her babies are emptied

like pockets of sea men
who abandoned their ships to uncover
sand's grey land. Their jackets
unravel, bared to old threading,
their hands are unfolding like clams
craving shedding.

We mourn those who leave us
while we are asleep, unfind those remnants
they left us to keep, bury in earth
precious gems for those waking,
gather our sticks to make new
what is shaking.

She is only and always in search
of a nest—

As if daybreak were coming
and the weary could soon rest,
she presses old wind against
her small held breath.

If Hunger Persuades

They're going to the circus,
the circus starts at eight.

Blue fabric
on her thin body

runs back and back
along tracks, retracing steps

and gaps in her dress,
back stooped with age

or crazed, downward-looking
hunger, feet feeling dirt and grass,

clouds eager to swallow
the earth whole.

For hours the right side lighter
than the left, I know

the name
of this road,

its number, too,
and its curves, hills,

swallows where a truck
almost hit, where a truck did

hit a small woman with bent knees,
face down, breathing.

Driving in
like flying over

I descend
onto the tips

of light, balance my weight
between halves, watch

the clouds near me
darkness near

enough to stick out
my tongue, fearing

sky facing dusk,
dawn, changings

like fire to wax (I squeeze)
my own hand

creases in the dark.

At These Limits

When I looked up, the priest
was gone and another round man
had taken his place.
When this one prayed
he put his feet together,
clasped his eyes, pressed
his ears back.
Next door, she fastened
her hands to her waist
and sent away envelope
after envelope
which were clinging
to her carpeted floor.
We wend our weary way,
disrobing, unmounting, covering—
I have not taken milk
from the mouths
of children. I am swallowing
the earth, however,
and it is ripe and clean
and spills down my chin.

Prophets

The men left in water
grimace and float,

mutter to themselves
about Warsaw

a little mob, they knew
who was a Jew and who

wasn't. Little kids,
they were just—

After us, there
will be no one

to remember and do
you speak Hebrew?

Unsettled, one
wraps his head

in cotton against
Florida sun

coming for white
skin, story.

A little, yes
and in my mind

they stare hopefully
at me, bare

shoulders, pale
blue eyes

from the Cossack
and waiting for

my turn. But they
are bitter, bored

and this is just
talk for a hot

winter's day when
it's too bright

to look
beyond the closest

faces and stretch
past our own life.

Many to Remember

Break slate. Break marble. Break bread
over the sink. Break chimes, break glass, break time
in pieces like fingernails. Break blades
of grass, break glory (don't laugh). Break
the oven and burn the toast. Break a person and
watch it melt. (The breaking is *it*.)
Break a ceramic plate, break the broom,
break the dustpan, watch the house
gather stones. Break the statue's hand,
break the mother's hand, break salt
over potatoes. Break in cycles,
break in patterns like plaid. Break snow,
break fall, break the fast
and watch the Torah
fall to the floor. Break windows,
break walls, break rocking chairs, break fingers.
Break spontaneity, break language, break dough and
bake it outside. Break the tent, break the wood,
break the matches in thirds, sit cold.
Break skin with tattoos, with numbers, with
labels. Break codes, break Eichmann, watch the trial
of evil's left hand. Break through,
break free, break under barbed wire,
break up into the sky.

New Origin Myth

And so and then and so then of
these six we will take five
and we will grow them
to be seven.

《◆|||◆》
Myth Expands

At the beginning of time, angels danced with children danced with wind danced with sky. Myth expands to include all those who came before.

(Flush Inspired)

"It must be admitted that there are
very few authorities for the foregoing biography."
        —*Flush: A Biography,* Virginia Woolf

The man with yellow gloves
is also a monkey, but not really,
or at least, not every day.

Each morning he buttons his jacket
and straightens his shoes,
one for each foot,

and he walks down the street
swinging his umbrella back and forth,
rain or shine.

The beetle on its back
in the middle of the pavement
isn't noticed by the man

or the world,
both calm and swaying.
The beetle is thinking

its hardest thoughts
of mortality, physics, feet.
The man is displacing language,

both of the past and of another,
rhyming angels with candles
and islands with silence.

The angels are coming down

to the beetle, wondering
whether to flip his body

or carry him up their stairs,
one angel to each leg.
The man will never witness

a sight like this; he certainly
doesn't see this one.
His umbrella waves to the day,

each pleat folding stored words
which he mumbles as he walks,
as he greets the bright morning,

crunches underneath his straight shoes.

Illusion!

Look out! The electricity is dripping
sticky tar on your shoulders!

The town's first wedding was met
with sparks on linen, full-dress

drill, the bride beside herself, crazed joy
on her face all night. Look out!

What you saw has turned,
light bulb caving in

on its glass dome drawing,
melted snow, forks and knives

across the floor. Over there,
a weeping willow sucking in light

to spit at its neighbor. Over there,
a tile shop, lit up by oil and

insistent of its past, walls, windows
sealed-up ceramic. Imagine shattering

a glass globe of the earth, green pieces
fall down, blue pieces go up

to greet blue eyes
pierce, blink, have

we survived?

Idols in the Desert

Past prayer
  plead
  passivity.

God's Desert

Who are these farmers
and what do they think
of me, my silver car

halting across arid
asphalt, water mirages
at every bend.

We pass through
mammoth country, the burning
bush, petrified forests, all this

from waking. Free samples
in this desert, take the sand
in jars, sleds, desert eyes

see inside you, though, have
you groomed? Showered
last night, different state,

harsher sun, the bush now
aflame, could I be
a new Moses

seeing through, God,
is it you, your smiling
backside, why can't I stop seeing

this, idolatry, at first
I thought it silly, now I know
what those thinkers

were stuck on, wandering
through, to, see
the sunset over these mountains?

We could drive
endlessly, still
the light would not warm us

entirely, searingly
enough?

The Shul in Chelm

A shammes, a shabbes-
klapper, and a
shabbes-keeper
walk into a bar.

They spent their day
knocking on
shutters to let others
know they could

come in (leading to
legs cascading
over windowsills,
a mess).

They ground
the pepper, killed
the chicken, groomed
the floors.

The peppers were red
and yellow, plump,
the chicken was two
scrawny crows, the

broom was blown
by a gaffer. The bars
of the shul crumble under
steps (on the roof—

men dancing),
wood comes crashing
down. Luckily, the chickens
were already dead,

the peppers dashed,
the floors dreary.
They turns out to be
one man, heroic,

and the falling
timber only opens
the house to the sky,
yellow sun setting

above children's upturned eyes,
shammes scrambling
to capture the light
in his barrel.

Reflection over Winter

The swamp across the street has been cleared and so, if I walk through the brush and bend way over, I can see my face in the water. But it is winter and windy and so my face, like the big, white house, is blurry and creased. The house's flat walls look shingled, my forehead is wrinkled and small. The vulture is circling again and when it blocks the sun and then swoops down, flashes of light illuminate my reflection. The swamp is cooing, drawing me closer, drawing me in. I am wading and I look old. The branches and moss are beginning to grow back around its edges. The flies are beginning to buzz again above the surface. Soon, it will all be covered, the water mostly hidden. I am unsure where I will be when this comes. The air is crisp and cold, the wind is on my neck, the sound of branches leaning over swamp, slowly creaking and then settling, is pulsing, just barely, just there. The vultures are on the roof, spreading their wings. The sun is beginning to swallow them whole.

Collecting Samples

We know little
of what is beside us
who lies beside us
under dark blue light

kitchen's searing walls
sharpen as eyes yearn,
flinch, head dulled
into fabric and flesh

petrified wood shutters
away daylight
we remain
veined

slowly changing
barely bearing
the weight
of our new skin

Burial

The sky is too bright without birds.
Eight small figures in the middle of a green field,
crops up to their waists, in different colored shirts,
trucks parked at the edge of the road, walk
toward the cars, trudging as if
through thick water, as if
they were dropped in the middle and are surprised
they must find their way out.

≪•IV•≫
Archive's Tales

We enter the past, try to unearth. Words coo, retreat—I am stealing, they are listening, waiting to see what tools I'll use for my thievery. Or, they're longing to arrive, and I am chosen.

Mothers of language—when you gathered your words, did the stories survive? What I take, I remake.

Manuscript

Extended palm
inscribed
flower, cross
in oval frame

extend this
skin to find
ground, minerals
beet and barley

fleshed like
fables that craft
and crawl along
slopes, scripts

hand writing scrawls—
one came, one
leapt before
the sun grew tall

(of those who've written
these this
renewal, ink
and line, is

barely pressed
under different
stamp) flapping
her wings the dove

begins to wail,
can I catch
her song as
she falls

Archive's Tales I

The forest quakes at
three, birds scatter
soil frees
its tree roots
and loose trunks
go bounding toward water.

Under the flesh
of Sedona mountains
ladybugs and worms
marry, grow
old. Those
of us above
ground leave
footprints on
their chuppahs, mar
their birthdays with
half-hearted calls.

Too much space, say
those who listen beneath
and dislike voice
as it travels. Too much
space between what
we speak and
what our quivering
mouths demand.

Archive's Tales II

We talk above stretched
linen, barely
words to pass
back and forth,
while those who wrote
long before
dug through soil
to make, fleshed
their minds into forms
latent, awaiting, watered,
then arrived.

We live our instincts through
story and the language
of the earth chimes back
we are nearing
that which came before.

Animal Markings

The geese arrive with teeth
bared, latching like children
onto ducks' sucked coats.
Log upturned resembles flesh
pecking at lights
flashing by, tails
wagging above water.

The goose's wings are latched
on to the sky, her blue
threaded through.

The man is lost
in the way
(by) now, brush-beat stone
and beaten part
on her soft head.
He could have left
her (whole).

The baby's skull splits
at its sunk seams,
he has captured
what she was,
left her un-
earthed;
a quarter (reward)
arrives at his front door,
along with a feather

along with a feathered pen
along with a card
on which
he can inscribe his name.

Unearth

"and a holy wilderness
Has sunk roots, where much is being readied"
— "The Titans," Friedrich Hölderlin

Freight train rumbles soil, displaces petals
under leaves, branches stack as if

by hand. Wind falls through
open seams, cross-stitched, sounds

echo beneath. Under this, damp earth
rich with worm eggs, marks where footprints

scarred, faint light inside the black. All of this
winding through, passing and pushing

aside, stone changes in lined rock,
crystallized underbellies, I reach

my hand down into and pull out weeds,
willow branches, cacti needles,

bark of each continent, tree rings with dinosaur
hands stamped in, petrified, recoil,

not Earth, only I, pressing dirt
between my fingers, earth falling

changed and unamused, glinting
its eyes to tell me

it is beyond
grasp.

Holy Wilderness

Near the beginning, rooting ash,
unburied dead, radiant light.

Before this, sea and voice
rising and falling to dusk. As

the calling subsides, sounding earth
hums, ushering in

tide and wave, shore passed
and formed anew.

And before this,
silence? Our God,

slowly making, remaking,
inventing our colors, all

in quiet. After, color
gains sound, reaps

orange, rips blue,
shattering of every

kind, noise and
taste. Stores of lead

and leavening steel,
daily collapse. Soon,

paralysis, tree trunks frozen
in steep ice, whispers

stuck in shrinking
caves, can you hear

the echo, slowly turning
into a long

drone, syncopation
hiccupping. Return—

wilderness holied
and waiting for sound

that won't vanish
upon arrival, waiting for sea

and fable to join at last,
salty linens overlay

glass, radiant script
wet, glinting, sees

the sounds we leave.

Archive's Diction

Fossils store, then restore
the sounds we've forgotten
how to speak.

Mornings underneath
birds' flight, our shadows
on the sidewalk, muted,

we sit. Listen,
we can get closer,
closer to where

animals chant, parade,
fill the air
with new life.

The sleeping sounds
are coming, daring
to cross
into this world

unburdened.

‹‹• V •››
Behind the Brush

Here, I'm at the edge of these voices.
I have heard inside others—what now do I make?

Translation

At the edge of words
I accompany you, seeing.
What you put in this earth
comes in letters, parts,
apart from what I take—
my truth of tradition, ascending,
adjacent—your wisdoms
cling, prosper, yet exceed
their means, unable to sieve
the past's near ending
and my nearing
to you, alphabet
gardened, growing,
holding its fullness, I come
to provide, print these knowings
and follow your sufferings
from where they came.

He Fell Again

He fell again
this time at a concert
last time at shul
or that was the other

grandfather, Grandpa,
though Zede fell, too
his nose crooked
they are letting it be.

His wife is tired
fell down after
a kitchen collision
he didn't mean

to knock her over
but the daughters
are still angry.
Grandpa's wife

a decade younger
than the others
wonders what she will do
soon, her sister, husband,

ninety. When they fall,
it must be unlike
when I fell, in hot summer
or after a blood test

in my dad's young
arms, for them
it is fear, ambulance men
through the door, heavy coats

coaxing them
into a white chair
to check vitality,
if someone told me

they were checking
my vitality I would
assume I was already
vitally lost and look around

on the floor
for my missing
pulses, maybe next to
my white shoes

by the door
or the condo's mailboxes.
I try to send them mail
once a month

to make the trips down-
stairs worthwhile, they said
it made their trips
worthwhile, I love

each of them
differently.
If I were too old
to tie my shoes

I would only
let my love
see me in the mornings.
They can all

tie their shoes, in fact,
they go to concerts
cook chickens and
meat loafs, spam and eggs

young Grandma a gym
goer, Grandpa follows
along, his back,
knees, he sits and rests

on his way back up
on a Florida bench
near the lizards
and when I'm there

he points as each goes by
and pulls my nose
and concernedly gives advice
every so often but otherwise

we chatter, make up
new noises, and he
is entirely sane
but we find insanity

together works best
and relieves
back pain and worries
he has one cousin

a month older
and they exchange calls
and birthday cards and I
wonder who will

survive me.

Cossacks Coming

Cozying cossacks crawl
cringing through wet
gall, piped tobacco, flint
and tone. Seagulls call

or hack, their rote
paths learned
from birth, silt
and silks

hide under hearth. Swing
from plant to plant, little
fledglings fall
to earth.

Zede, *Rachel*

I wonder of God
and my good fortunes
blessed life
makes you almost
religious, a bridge
on Howard Street
along the edge
I fell from trees
how tall, how many
and before or since
unchanged, my mind
my companion
mine too
I ran through streets
to our nanny, got hit
by a car, hit my ear
can you see it?
in Germany we
were well-off
with a nanny
man below
selling beer, two alleys
and a moon
following
didn't I have this thought
too, am I like you?
me across alleys
I was smart
even then
a blessed life

Since the stroke
I'm sure you're wondering
please, I am not,
let's dwell, let's
recall
I will tell you
all I know
of my brain and its
tremor, this is how
a brain works
fine, you can explain
so I can see
you still can
I'll begin logically
and end
with logical
conclusions
good, good, now back
to the cars,
cross-country, cross-
ocean, statue
from boat's prow
your father and mother
stoics, your laughter,
the dishware through
glass, cell, border
jail, boat, border
I'll explain from the
beginning, I can see
you understand
I'll hold these

you are feeding
me, I love
when you know
me as you
I have led a blessed life
you will make much
of this world, I wish
you will see it
I will conjure
like you conjure
portraits of parents
on the walls
they bought this house
for its walls
There's something I don't know
will never know, that's as far
as I get
you've gone far
farther than I
can go, (cannot envy,
Rachel, do not envy)
boats, borders
only in your stories
glass out the window
we are
as far
as we can get

Behind the Brush

The yellow house woman
over reservoir and coyote calls
had all the markings
of a land, gritted *hush*
to dawn dogs barking
as they warned her
of their findings. Over here,

inside the dust, God
can hide me, smell
me, fuss.

God sees me behind the brush

language-stealer, landscape-
bearer, scrolls on my back
rolled and replaced,
I am fearing
my own.

Libro de Cordilleras

I must have something to say
about worm hole branches
cut into brown-bound, leather-
sated book-creased
ink drawings intended
as letters

Holes no absence
or presence, shaped as fish,
hats, trees and leaves,
arrowed fences,
promised and promising:

Dot line dot bleed
pig fire flee

My grandfather again
white glass blue sea

On his couch, we are
just there
knowing

the curve of the hills
line dot free

Epilogue

On the sea, and we sang unto You

—Berakhot 14b:10

[re-]Exodus

Covenant and salt   alphabetic acrostic   lamedh lamedh
the taste of theft   north to south [aligned]   standing prayer
bowing prayer   stiffly rise   slowly rise
rise up   in awe   fear [shame]

There is a bird   in the cities   by the sea
and when the sun   rises   changes colors

[a missing word, leap to]

captivity   of the land   as it was   in the beginning
rebuild ruins [but] regain   sorrow   bird circling   ahead
we only remember   those sorrows just   passed [mostly, luckily
or   burden]

When is God angry?
When the rooster   sun wailing   white   on one leg

Between the pillars   pray   this is not difficult
broken vessels   deserve shelf space   like older people
who have lost   [wit] knowledge
remember them   well

sky-blue and white
sky-blue and leek- green

Sing, barren woman
for your song   will withstand [surpass]   [your] barrenness

Light rolling away   bundle your songs
into one   which remembers
old as new   [as] what is gone   what is coming

[align] exodus   from Egypt   in the dark
with new darknesses   lifting sand   each day
bared   harder now   to recall
only our last   sorrow

NOTES

Observant Marranos

    Beginning in the fifteenth century, Marranos, *converted Jews, fled the Iberian Peninsula and the Spanish Inquisition and journeyed to Mexico, where they established Jewish and Jewish-Christian communities. In a pamphlet from 1944, published by the American Friends of the Mexican Indian Jews, a visitor to a community in Mexico wrote that the* marranos *feel a connection to Jewish tradition because of "'The Call of the Blood' deep-seated in their souls." This poem interrogates that phrase.* Marranos *is a derogatory word, utilized into the twentieth-century by American scholars, which loosely translates to mean "pig."*

Inquisition Letters

    While in prison in Mexico City, Luis de Carvajal, a crypto-Jew who would soon be executed for his sustained Jewish practices by the Mexican Inquisition, sent letters to his sisters which he inscribed inside fruits and vegetables. Luis de Carvajal el Mozo has been memorialized as a martyr.

Me'am Lo'ez

    The Me'am Lo'ez, *an anthology of commentaries on the Torah, was written in Ladino by ten different authors across 166 years in the Ottoman Empire. The first edition of the text, devoted to Genesis, was written by Rabbi Ya'akov Khulí in 1730. In Genesis 1:4, Khulí wrote: "The light that remains in our world is merely a seventh of the light that existed during the days of creation. Some say that this primeval light was 60,075 times as bright as the light of the sun."*

The Myth of la Llave

The myth of la llave *appears in New Mexico crypto-Jews' oral histories as well as propagandistic documents of the Spanish government. The myth claims that in 1492, during expulsion, converted Jews took the keys to their Spanish houses along with the hope that they would one day return. These keys, according to the myth, still lie hidden in cabinets and bedside tables. According to many New Mexico crypto-Jews, the swallow serves as a symbol of the expelled Jew.*

Mother of Exile

Emma Moya, a New Mexico crypto-Jew, created an extensive collection of Jewish memorabilia—poems, photographs, linguistic charts, newspaper clippings, genealogies—which is held in an archive in Albuquerque. Golondrina *translates to "swallow."*

God's Desert

When Moses asks God, "Show me now Your ways, that I may know You" (Ex. 33:13), God answers: "I will make all My goodness pass before you" (Ex. 33:18). According to Maimonides, God allowed Moses to see His characteristics, His good ways and actions, His backside, but not His face.

The Shul in Chelm

The fictional town of Chelm, placed in Eastern Europe, reveals a nearby form of myth-making situated within Ashkenazi Jewish identity. The "Wise Men of Chelm" stories are often read to children before they go to sleep and tell tales of the town's foolish women and men.

Libro de Cordilleras

Libro de Cordilleras *is a leather-bound volume of ecclesiastical communications from nineteenth-century Mexico. Its pages have been carved out in places by bookworms. Written in various hands, the book contains letters on church doctrine, canon laws, and news.*

[re-]Exodus

This poem includes borrowed and modified lines from Berakhot (Blessings), *a text composed in Talmudic Babylon (450-550 CE) and belonging to the first order,* Zera'im (Seeds), *of the Talmud. Berakhot discusses the rules of blessings and prayers, including the Shema and the Amidah.*

ABOUT THE AUTHOR

RACHEL BERNSTEIN KAUFMAN is currently pursuing a PhD in Jewish and Latin American History at UCLA. Her poetry has appeared on poets.org and in the *Harvard Review, Southwestern American Literature, Western Humanities Review, JuxtaProse,* and elsewhere, and her prose has appeared in *The Yale Historical Review* and *Rethinking History.* She received a BA in English and History from Yale University.

For the full Dos Madres Press catalog:
www.dosmadres.com